Original title:
Life's Meaning: For Sale (Cheap)

Copyright © 2025 Creative Arts Management OÜ
All rights reserved.

Author: Clara Whitfield
ISBN HARDBACK: 978-1-80566-123-8
ISBN PAPERBACK: 978-1-80566-418-5

Price Slashed Emotions

Feelings on clearance, don't you know?
Happiness bundled with a flat bow.
Once overpriced, now quite the deal,
Buy one, get one, how does it feel?

Joy on sale, with a small dent,
Sadness returning, it's well spent.
Glimmers of laughter, discount delight,
Grab your emotions, they're flying, take flight!

Rediscovered Reveries

Daydreams found under couch debris,
Imaginary worlds, two for a fee.
Laughter echoes in bargain bins,
With whimsy on sale, where fun begins.

Thoughts up for barter, trade a few smiles,
Wandering minds running miles and miles.
There's magic in chaos, or so they say,
It's much more fun when you're lost along the way!

Cost-Benefit Phantoms

Ghosts of choices, haunting your mind,
A deal too tempting, hard to leave behind.
Calculating joy, subtracting the dread,
I bought happiness but got dread instead.

Phantoms of laughter, or was that a scream?
One dollar dreams, how absurd they seem.
Prices rising on wisdom, what a strange game,
Still, I keep playing, 'cause who's really to blame?

Priceless Moments

Moments mistaken for a yard sale find,
Little giggles tangled, humor entwined.
We hand out smiles, with a dollar's grace,
Unwrap the joy, make a funny face.

Silly snapshots, what a great score,
Buy one moment, get three more!
Cherish these treasures, silly and bright,
Priceless hilarity, holding hands tight!

Dreams on Consignment

In a shop of wishful thinking,
Dreams hang like coats on a rack.
Buy one, get another free,
But they never seem to come back.

Check the price tag for a giggle,
Offered at half the price of hope.
Return for a refund if you wiggle,
The checkout line is a slippery slope.

The Thrift of Time

Tick-tock, the clock's on sale,
Buy yesterday, get tomorrow too.
Plan out your life, don't leave a trail,
But the hours seem to bid adieu.

Grab a bargain on those memories,
They're slightly used, but who will care?
Just don't misplace the reveries,
As clearance items linger in air.

Collecting Change for Simplicity

Pocket lint and dreams collide,
A penny saved is a regret,
I'll buy a smile, it's ratified,
With every dime, no debt, no debt!

Lend me your worries, I'm up for trade,
I'll give you laughter, just one for one.
With each jingle, I'm surely swayed,
Selling joy under the sun.

Ending the Bidding War

Once at the auction of the absurd,
Bids were flying, wild and free.
I raised my hand, in a silly word,
But no one wanted my heartfelt fee.

Sold to the highest faux pas!
For a song and a dance, what a thrill.
The crowd erupted in mirth and awe,
As I bought back my doubts with a quill.

Yard Sale Wisdom

In a box, truths are piled high,
A rubber chicken, oh my, oh my!
Faded dreams in haggled packs,
Each price tag offers some silent cracks.

Twelve cents for hopes, a nickel for glee,
Buy one regret, and get two for free!
Life's grand lessons, slightly used,
At yard sales, we're all amused.

Pallet of Possibilities

Stacked high with laughter, stacked low with dread,
A pallet of choices, on which we tread.
Pick a path, but watch for dust,
Some decisions rust, while others combust.

Chose a mug that screams, "Live Your Best Day!"
Next to it, a sign that says, "Just Take It Away!"
Bubble wrap dreams, float just out of reach,
What's worth more? The lesson, or the speech?

Empty Shelves of Desire

On empty shelves, wishes sit in lines,
A toaster without bread, a riddle with signs.
Two rubber ducks wait for company,
"Pick us, pick us!" they honk in harmony.

A bottle of hope, with half-empty cheer,
Next to a clock that forgot to steer.
Desires wrapped in mismatched pairs,
Sometimes sold with a side of stares.

Thrifted Insights

From thrifted truths, wisdom shines bright,
A cat-shaped lamp glowing through the night.
Each quirky find tells a tale untold,
In colors mismatched, stories unfold.

A sweater that shrunk with some lingering dreams,
And coffee-stained pages of philosophical schemes.
Digging through junk for a nugget of fun,
In a world of the silly, we've already won.

Tags Torn Off the Present

A tag once read, 'Best gift you'll see,'
But now it's lost, oh woe is me!
I wrap it up, with bows so bright,
Yet still it whispers, it's not quite right.

A coupon here for joyful days,
But who's the buyer? Who pays?
It's marked down twice, the joke's on us,
The perfect gift, just lacks the fuss.

Redistributing Value

I found a penny, shiny and new,
Marked as treasure in a grand view.
I placed it proudly on my shelf,
Perhaps it's worth more than myself!

A dollar bill from yesterday's fun,
Is now a relic, or just a pun?
What's high today could drop like cheese,
As price tags flutter in the breeze.

Timeless Trinkets

I bought a clock, but it won't tick,
A timeless piece, or just a trick?
It hangs there laughing, frozen in time,
Reminding me I paid a dime!

A rubber chicken, bright and loud,
Is worth much more than a silver shroud.
It bounces back with every jest,
In life's great sale, it's truly blessed.

Pricey Lessons

I grabbed a book, its cover torn,
Each lesson learned, a little worn.
They say 'Buy wisdom,' what a steal!
But turning pages, what's the deal?

A fortune spent on silly tales,
Yet through the laughs, true wisdom sails.
The pricey lessons, oh what fun,
When all's said and done, we've already won!

Sale of the Soul

Got a soul in mint condition,
Only used on sunny days.
It dances and hums a tune,
Perfect for a life that sways.

Package deals on laughter,
Throw in some quirky charm.
Trade it all for a good pun,
Why not? It can't cause harm!

Bring your best offer here,
With a smile, you won't regret.
Even a bit of dread,
Some wisdom for your pet.

Hurry now, don't delay,
Tick-tock, the clock does chime.
Take my heart, it's just for laughs,
Heartache's out, it's sale time!

In Search of Authenticity

Looking for the real deal,
Not just dusty old talk.
A vintage vibe, a good feel,
Something that can truly rock.

I saw a sign down the lane,
"Authentic smiles for sale!"
But they looked a bit plain,
Might just be an old tale.

A moment of high comedy,
For this price, who can resist?
Grab your quirks, a good spree,
Check the list and don't get missed.

Searching for what feels true,
But laughter's where I land.
Here's a joke, a funny view,
Swapping tales is just so grand!

Salvaging Significance

In the clearance bin of thought,
I found meaning next to shoes.
Dusty dreams all tangled, caught,
But worth it in the views.

Smiles here, it's half off today,
Old regrets, one for a dime.
Grab some joy along the way,
Laughter's always in its prime.

Mismatched socks of value seem,
Each holds stories to unpack.
Here's a purpose—wait, it's green—
Oh well, just put it back!

Salvaging what life can lend,
With a twist of comedic flair.
Finding gold, a quirky friend,
Is that meaning? Who's to care?

Choices in Clearance

Choices stacked in neat rows,
Buy one smile, get one free.
Select your path, nobody knows,
Which one has the best glee?

Pick a kit to mix and match,
Happiness on the shelf.
Grab a design without a scratch,
It's fun to choose for self!

Here's a coupon for some chuckles,
With every laugh, you win.
Discounts on those silly rumbles,
Who knew fun's now a sin?

Grab the offers, don't you wait,
This clearance ends at noon.
Choose wisely, don't hesitate,
Enjoy your time… and cartoon!

Sale Sign in the Mind

Thoughts on sale, get them here,
Discounted dreams, fold and clear.
Buy one truth, get a lie,
Hurry now, don't let it slide!

Find your wishes, half-off price,
Bargain feelings, roll the dice.
Special offer on your dreams,
Act fast—nothing's as it seems!

Counting Change for Purpose

Pennies dropped in purpose's jar,
Quarters wasted, what a bar!
A dollar for a smile today,
Just to chase the blues away!

Nickels spent on idle chat,
Counting thoughts, where's my hat?
Dimes for wisdom, six for fun,
Look at me, I'm feeling done!

Clearance Rack of History

Old regrets on rack display,
Marked down memories lead astray.
"Buy now—bring your baggage too!"
No refunds on what once was you.

Special price for ancient tales,
Haunted past, with bargain sales.
Just one session, take a seat,
With every blunder, laugh's complete!

The Cost of Contentment

Price tag reads: 'Settle down,'
Bargain basements wear the crown.
Fleeting joy, it's on the shelf,
Buy a friend, just be yourself!

Priceless laughs, a bargain spree,
Grab your happiness for free!
Happy hour on sunny days,
For more, just smile in odd ways!

Labels and Limitations

In a store with signs so bright,
They sell dreams, oh what a sight!
Grab a label, squeeze it tight,
But can it truly feel just right?

Discount souls on every shelf,
Bargains marked to please yourself.
Need a purpose? Buy a crown,
Just remember, don't fall down!

The True Cost of Happiness

Joy on sale, but what's the price?
Do we barter with our vice?
A laughter heard through petty deals,
Platinum smiles, but broken feels.

What's the checkout for your grin?
Cash or credit? Where to begin?
Pay in tears or trade with sass,
All for that fleeting hourglass!

Purpose on Clearance

Today's special: find your soul,
For half-off, it's quite the goal!
Stacked high with dreams, oh what a mess,
Can purpose fit in this dress?

Grab a cart, roll through the aisle,
Each item wrapped with a quirky smile.
Some might fit, some are just fluff,
Finding meaning can be quite tough!

Unpriced Thoughts

Thoughts unpriced, a mystery yet,
In a box that's old and wet.
Try to sell them; it's a hoot,
Buy one, get one—what's the loot?

A brainstorm's worth a penny's weight,
But salesmen laugh—they love the fate.
Whispers of wisdom, always a tease,
They're hand-me-downs, but won't you please?

Half-Price Soul Searching

In the bargain bin of dreams,
I find my thoughts like faded schemes.
Four dollars off for wisdom rare,
But wait, there's also free despair.

I try on joy, it fits too tight,
While hope is marked down, what a sight!
I ask for answers, they say 'Oops!'
Only slightly used, a couple scoops.

A coupon for a heart of gold,
But in my cart, the truths are sold.
Discounted laughs and momentary glee,
Still wondering if this is all for me.

I leave the store with bags of doubt,
Returning items, giving up, no rout.
The clearance aisle was quite a thrill,
But all I found was half-priced will.

The Price of Happiness

Happiness on sale, two for one,
With each purchase, there's still some fun.
Pick up a laugh, a smile or two,
But they expire, just like my shoe.

The checkout line is notably long,
As folks debate if they belong.
With every tick of the clock, more fear,
'Will the joy last, or disappear?'

Bargain deals on good vibes galore,
But who knows what's behind the door?
A friendly ghost or a landlord's frown,
Maybe there's free shipping to clown town!

I leave with bags, feeling quite spry,
Yet wondering if I just bought a lie.
Happiness might be on rebate,
But I'm still puzzled about my fate.

Lost in the Clearance Aisle

Wandering where the deals are best,
Searching for bliss, a simple quest.
The clearance aisle beckons, bright and loud,
But I grab regrets, too big a crowd.

I find a t-shirt that says 'Be Bold',
Yet it shrinks in warmth when the night turns cold.
A trinket promising joy in a box,
But the warranty's gone — well, what a paradox!

Socks with stripes, a random book,
Each item whispers, 'Come take a look.'
But emptiness lurks between the lines,
No refund policy on lost designs.

As I wheel away my loaded cart,
I ponder if they sell a happy heart.
Maybe next time, I'll shop with care,
Not just for bargains, but with some flair.

Sale Ends Tomorrow: Decide Quickly

The sign is bright, a flashing light,
'Buy happiness now, it's quite a sight!'
But deep within, I sense a catch,
What price to pay for a tiny batch?

Skimming through options, feels like a race,
Do I want joy from the green jar or the vase?
One says 'Serenity' — the other 'Fun',
Grab both, and hope I won't come undone.

I check my wallet — not much space,
So I argue with sadness, a fierce face.
'Can I get two-for-one on makin' cheer?'
But sadness laughs, 'I've always been here!'

The salesman's grin is wide, so sly,
As he offers a hope that's hard to buy.
Before I know, I'm out the door,
With a handful of dreams and a wish for more.

Thrift Store Truths

In bins of odd bits, we search for gold,
Old shoes with stories, too shy to be told.
A mug with a chip, but it still holds brew,
Each find tells a tale, if only we knew.

A shirt with a stain, but who really cares?
It's perfect for days of running downstairs.
Faded jeans with patches, they laugh in delight,
Reminding us all to wear what feels right.

The Value of a Whisper

A whisper's like silk, so smooth and so light,
It dances through air, a secret in flight.
In crowded rooms, all the chatter's a mess,
But a quiet word holds the ultimate jest.

Price tags on feelings? A bargain or theft?
For hugs are for sale, and I'm not quite bereft.
So bid with a smile, don't let laughter stall,
The thoughts that we share, they are worth it all.

Markdown on Memories

Memories on sale, half off for today,
Like socks with odd pairs, they still find a way.
Some come with a tag that says 'Use with care,'
While others are vintage, with stories to share.

Time's like a clearance, it's fast and it flies,
We barter in moments, wear smiles, not lies.
So roll back the prices, enjoy the charm,
For laughter is priceless, and that's the best balm.

Secondhand Secrets

Secrets for sale, just a dime for a peek,
In boxes of whispers, so playful and sleek.
We find out the truths hidden deep in the racks,
With every new gossip, we put on our acts.

So try on the tales, they might just fit right,
Some sparkle like diamonds, while others take flight.
A treasure trunk full of quirks can be fun,
So grab one, take home, and let laughter run.

Frugal Reflections

In a thrift store of thoughts, I roam,
Seeking wisdom where dust has grown.
Price tags on dreams, just a dime,
Who knew insight was such a crime?

Penny for your thoughts, that's the deal,
Bargains on joy, how do you feel?
A dollar for laughter, what a laugh—
Life's a clearance sale on a broken path.

Old shoes, old laughs, worn-out dreams,
Wrapped up in fuzzy store-bought seams.
Here's a coupon for feeling fine,
Expiration soon, so grab your line!

So here I stand, a coupon king,
Trading moments for a plastic ring.
I'll buy a smile, but here's the glitch—
No refunds on love, so scratch that itch!

Value Tags on Feelings

Emotions on shelves, a curious sight,
Everything priced under fluorescent light.
Happiness marked down, a special treat,
Why is sadness sold at such a steep?

I found a frown, just a quarter spent,
But joy's a bit pricey; it's heaven sent.
Anger's on clearance, half-off today,
I'll take two bags, then throw them away!

Stock up on hope, it's fresh and new,
Love's always out of reach, it's true.
Grab a cart, let's roll through the aisles,
Collecting the gems mixed in with the wiles.

I'll haggle with fate for a dream or two,
But it seems the best things are never on cue.
So I'll take my chances, let laughter ring,
And pay for my lessons with a good ol' zing!

The Worth of a Tear

A tear's just a penny when placed on a scale,
Who knew such emotions could ever prevail?
Choking back laughter while pricing my dread,
Tears 2 for a nickel, sweet deals for my head.

We measure our pain in crude little jars,
Hoping for value from fate's racing cars.
Why is it cheap when I'm feeling blue?
Oh wait, my joy's underpriced too!

I'll sell you my worries, they come in a pack,
Trade them for giggles, feel free to snack.
So pass me a chuckle, I'll toss you a sigh,
Let's barter our burdens, we'll laugh till we cry!

Collecting emotions like trinkets and charms,
Gluing together our carefully worn arms.
So if you've a tear, just know it's a find,
They're worth far more than the price you assign!

Garage Sale of Ideals

Welcome to my garage, ideals must go,
Bargains on values like 'give and take' flow.
I'll trade you a notion for just a small fee,
Or a warm hug for a cup of plain tea.

Here's a vision, slightly used,
A dream that's a bit bewildered and bruised.
Pick it up quick, it's a vintage delight,
Though its fabric is frayed, it still fits just right!

I've got aspirations, the clearance 'right now',
Throw in a wish, and I'll take a bow.
So barter your tales in this quirky bazaar,
Just don't haggle too hard, I'm not raising the bar!

But what's this? A smile, it's 50% off!
Better grab it quick; it's the best kind of scoff!
So come and join me; we'll trade and we'll spin,
In this whimsical sale where all joy can begin!

Bartering with Fate

I offered my heart, she asked for my shoes,
A trade of good fortune for less than good news.
I haggled with ghosts and even with time,
But the price of true wisdom? It doesn't rhyme.

I tossed in my worries, a bundle or two,
She laughed and said, "Honey, they're worthless to me.
But I've got a fortune cookie, in crispy old parchment,
Would you like to learn if it's more fun to be free?"

I bartered my patience, my sense of decorum,
She wrapped in a smile, but it felt like a quorum.
"Let's call it a deal, enjoy the free show,
After all, my dear, aren't we just here for the glow?"

With laughter and quirks, I walked out the door,
Who knew that fate's game could be such a bore?
The residue of hope stuck like gum on my shoe,
While my dreams of a bargain still felt fresh and new.

Life's Yard Sale

At the yard sale of being, where dreams are for sale,
I found a few echoes and a dust-covered tale.
I picked up a giggle, it only cost a dime,
Tossed in a sigh, said, "Hey, that's sublime!"

I grabbed a sad story, it was missing a page,
Patted a grumpy old clock, said, "You're all the rage!"
I tripped on my past, it was marked at a loss,
Then found a bright future, wrapped up in my gloss.

The banner read happiness, just hanging by tape,
I offered my struggles, as though they were grapes.
The lady with laughter, she shook her head sweet,
"Darling, my dear, now that's not a great feat!"

With treasures collected, I carried them home,
A mosaic of moments, the mind loves to roam.
In the yard sale of life, it seems things are cheap,
If we laugh at the chaos, we'll never lose sleep.

The Last Remaining Dream

In the clearance of wishes, one dream stood alone,
With a price tag that read, 'Try it, don't moan!'
I picked it up gently, like a fragile old toy,
Whispered, "Are you broken, or just being coy?"

The dream gave a chuckle, a twinkle, a grin,
"I'm waiting for someone to let me begin!
Slip into your heart, I promise it's neat,
Just buy me a latte, or maybe some sweet."

But what's the exchange, I wondered in doubt,
Is it worth all the fluff, or just filled with clout?
It hinted of laughter, of rainbows and glee,
So I tossed in a penny and screamed, "Set me free!"

Now I waltz on my dream, with its quirky delight,
Twisting and twirling, all through the night.
I traded my worries, a whimsical scheme,
For the last remaining laugh in this beautiful dream.

Discounted Smiles

At the store of bright feelings, where mood swings abound,
I found a few smiles that were marked way down.
They claimed to be happy, a humorous spree,
But most were expired, just waiting for free.

I picked up a wink, it was half off today,
A cheeky little nod, a well-rehearsed play.
I added a chuckle, still fresh on the rack,
And a sprinkle of joy that I'd never look back.

The cashier was grinning, a master of jest,
Said, "Choose wisely, dear friend, this sale is the best!
But don't buy too many, they're known to run out,
And laughs cost you dearly when you're full of doubt."

With smiles in my pocket, I skipped out the door,
Discounted and merry, what could I want more?
For in the great bargain of laughter and cheer,
I bought myself happiness, loaded with beer!

Clearance Sale on Ambitions

Dreams are marked down, just take your pick,
Once shiny and bright, now a little slick.
Achieve your goals, they're half off today,
Come and grab yours, don't let them stray.

Look to the shelves, see passions dusted,
Coupons for courage, isn't that rusted?
Won't you hurry, they're flying off racks,
While stocks last, avoid any hacks!

Giggles included, but costs start to rise,
Buy now, the fun's in the highs and the sighs.
But wait, there's a catch, a fee for the doubts,
Add to your cart, if you've got the clout!

So join the parade, it's a high-flying spree,
Where big hopes get sold, come see, come see!
Grab a good bargain, and don't be shy,
'Cause friends, funny fortune is passing you by!

Buy One, Get One Regret

Step right up, folks, don't miss this chance,
Buy one bold move, get a regret dance.
In this bright bazaar, options galore,
Each choice is a ticket, to never ignore.

With every decision, there's laughter and tears,
Grab a souvenir from your teenage years.
Swap a silly story for a slice of your pride,
Happiness guaranteed, or it's free on the side!

Two for the price of one, how could you resist?
A checklist of choices, just add to the list.
But be careful, my friend, it's a slippery floor,
With slippery decisions that could leave you sore!

So come take a ride on regret's merry-go-round,
Where ups and downs tumble and laughter is found.
Have fun with your fumbles, they just make you bright,
In this wild, wacky sale, you'll find delight!

Negotiating with Time

I called up the clock for a discount today,
"Dear Time, what's the price? Can we do it my way?"
"Just five years off, but two more in return,
A deal that's just perfect, if you dare to learn."

Tick-tock, the seconds, are stretching so thin,
Bartering moments, let the games begin!
"Add a latte, I'll throw in a laugh,
And a spare hour for your photograph."

Time said, "Bargains come wrapped in a wrinkle,
With every gain, a chance for a crinkle.
But rush not, my friend, take a moment or few,
Consider the offer before it's all due."

So dance with the seconds, go negotiate,
Time loves a jester who finds joy in fate.
Trade giggles for guidance, and breathe in the glee,
For each tick brings a chance, oh can't you see?

Thrifting for Truths

Welcome to the store where the truths are rare,
A bit dusty, but they've got plenty of flair.
Browse through the aisles, see wisdom in blue,
Faded opinions that still feel brand new.

Old notions stacked high with a price tag that's low,
Try one on, see if it fits your flow.
"Always be honest," says the truth with a wink,
"Or at least take a break, let the rest of us think."

Half-price beliefs, with a scratch or two,
Some come with stories, just waiting for you.
Bargain-bin morals, oh, what a delight,
You'll leave feeling wise, even if it's aight!

So sift through the junk, find gems shining bright,
In the thrift store of reasons, where all feel all right.
That's life, my good friends, a jumble of stuff,
Embrace what you find, that's the fun of the bluff!

Unseen Inventory

A box of dreams sits on the shelf,
Marked down because it watched itself.
A snicker, a wink, a deal too sweet,
Grab it quick before it's beat.

Philosophy comes in bags of chips,
Crumbs of wisdom on your lips.
Take a nibble, don't look back,
Thoughts are cheap, but fun's the knack.

Dance on shelves of half-priced glee,
A cartful of 'what might be.'
Of all the joys that could be found,
Pickles are deep thoughts, all around.

Life's puzzle offers odd-shaped pieces,
Find the ones that give you breezes.
A mix of laughter, tears on sale,
Choosing joy—you cannot fail.

Life in Discounted Chapters

Once upon a time, oh what a tale,
Discounted scripts that always fail.
Bargains on dreams that never land,
A plot twist that plays with your hand.

The hero's quest is in aisle five,
Where sock puppets strive to survive.
Take a detour, laugh at the booth,
Find cheap thrills instead of truth.

Pages dog-eared, stories collide,
Best-sellers resting, nowhere to hide.
So grab a cup with plots so odd,
Mix joy and chaos—it's all a facade.

Half-off dramas, romantic flops,
Moments turn into laughable hops.
Choose your adventure, come take a peek,
In this aisle of quirky, we're all unique.

The Shelf Life of Understanding

Knowledge on sale in jars from the past,
Open one lid, and you'll have a blast.
A sprinkle of wisdom, a dash of fear,
Concoctions of thought—better grab a cheer!

Levels of crazy in bright, bold hues,
Each canister holds the strangest views.
Bargains in insight dance with delight,
Who knew the shelf could be so light?

Expiration dates on thoughts so old,
Best before now, if truth be told.
Rip off the label for a taste so fine,
Life's quirks are waiting—in every line.

So shop for laughter, just take a chance,
In this reading cart, there's room to dance.
Grab nuggets of fun, leave the frown,
With each bend and curve, wear the crown.

Price Tags of Reflection

A sticker here reads 'deep and profound,'
Next to a joke that's barely sound.
Price tags offer a witty twist,
Be sure to check what you might miss.

Reflect on moments under bright lights,
Each tag a tale in endless fights.
The markup on joy is hard to gauge,
Check the clearance rack on every page.

Bargain bin thoughts in disarray,
Some spark laughter, others sway.
Punchlines pop and wisdom hides,
Peel back layers, see what resides.

Take home reflections, but beware the cost,
Each chuckle may leave something lost.
In the sale's hustle and joking spree,
Let's find the fun in "Just be free."

The Market of Meaning

In the market of dreams we barter and trade,
All the wisdom we've gathered, now ready to fade.
A bargain for joy, it's labeled 'half price',
But you'll need a good return policy for this slice.

Pick up a laugh, it's on clearance today,
Try on some hope, but it might lead you astray.
The vendor's a joker, with a wink and a grin,
"Buy one, get one—oh dear, where to begin?"

They sell all the secrets under one weary roof,
Like "Find yourself here!" or "Lose your belief!"
But as you sift through the junk, you might just uncover,
A fresh pack of joy, the ultimate treasure.

So enter the market, embrace all the fun,
Trade your uncertainties for a laugh or a pun.
Though meaning may shift, and desires may meld,
In this wacky bazaar, your spirit is held.

Haggling for Joy

Strolling through stalls of delight and dismay,
With an armful of dreams, I'm ready to play.
A smile for a nickel, a chuckle for free,
It's a game of exchange in this whimsical spree.

I offer my worries; they're marked up too high,
The vendor just chuckles, "Oh give it a try!"
He proffers a joke, complete with a grin,
"Negotiate laughter, let the fun begin!"

I'm haggling fiercely, my heart in a spin,
"Two puns for my frown, and a grin for the win!"
He nods in agreement, "Make it three for a cheer,
At this stall of affection, there's never a fear."

So barter your burdens, pry joy from despair,
Life's like a market, buyer beware.
Though prices may rise and fall with a sigh,
Haggling for joy is the ultimate high!

Outdated Aspirations

In the aisle of ambitions, they roll on the floor,
Half-priced pursuits, all '80s décor.
A box full of dreams marked down with a sneer,
"Buy yesterday's hopes, they're still selling here!"

A poster of passion, so brightly designed,
Outdated desire? Well, ain't that a find!
"Collect 'em all, folks!" the shopkeeper yells,
Be wary of wishes; they come with some bells.

I spot my own dreams, they've gathered some dust,
The price tag has faded; it's choking on rust.
"Why's joy in the clearance? I thought it was rare!"
"Ah, dear friend!" he chuckles, "It's a collector's affair."

So sift through the shelves of forgotten delight,
Trade yesterday's goals for a laugh that's in sight.
For even in dust, you might uncover a gem,
An outdated aspiration can still lead to zen.

Flash Sale on Tomorrow

Under the fluorescent bulbs, a sign blares 'Today!',
With arrows and banners all pointing one way.
A flash sale on dreams that are "Free with a grin,"
Bring in a question; take free laughter in.

Tomorrow's the darling they market with charm,
Promising more but often raising alarm.
"Get it while it's hot!" a loudspeaker declares,
'Cause tomorrow may vanish—like socks from a pair.

They package up happiness, shrink-wrapped with care,
"Open with a smile, and breathe in fresh air!"
But heed the fine print; it all comes at a cost,
For cheer can't be bottled; it's often quite lost.

So grab your enthusiasm and run down this lane,
Tomorrow's just a sale, but joy's not in vain.
For even if time slips like sand through our hands,
Laughing in sales, we're the best of all bands!

Restore and Renew

Once I found joy in a dollar bin,
A bargain on smiles, let the laughter begin.
Got a second-hand heart, still with some glee,
Polished it up—now it's shining for me.

In the thrift store of dreams, I rummaged around,
Picked up a few hopes that were half-price, I found.
A quirky old thought, with some spark in its eye,
Who knew that a giggle could mean to apply?

Out in the yard sale, they offered delight,
For twenty-five cents, I could leap to new heights.
A yardstick for measures of fun I could chase,
Paved pathways of joy across humor's wide space.

Now I'm wheeling and dealing with whims in my hand,
Trading regrets for a ripe slice of sand.
Life's nothing but laughter, on clearance each day,
Grab your discount on happiness—come have a play!

Half-Priced Paths

Strolled down a road marked with offers galore,
With signs that said happiness was always in store.
Bought a map to my dreams for a singe tin of sparks,
You'd think getting lost would be one of those perks.

On sale were the moments I tripped over bliss,
Sweet whispers of wisdom wrapped up in a kiss.
With a tag on each challenge at fifty percent,
I shopped for my choices with a smile that was bent.

Haggled with wishes, got discounts on time,
Bartered procrastination for rhythm and rhyme.
A clearance on worries, a markdown on strife,
Who knew that cheap laughter could brighten my life?

Now I'm always searching for deals in the fun,
Neglecting the burdens we'd rather not shun.
With half-priced adventures, I'm bouncing with glee,
Let's trade in our frowns for pure jubilee!

The Lost Art of Exchange

Once I listed my woes on a virtual fair,
Hoping to swap them for just a bit of fresh air.
A whimsy exchange, I charged pennies or a grin,
With every concession, a chuckle would win.

I offered my fears for a side of delight,
Sometimes they'd linger, and sometimes take flight.
The barter of laughter wasn't so tough,
It turns out a snicker is truly enough.

Found a lonely heart, placed a bid for some cheer,
Negotiated emotions, made giggles sincere.
With a handshake of joy, let's create a new trend,
Where frowns turn to frenzy, my playground, my friend.

In this bazaar of mishaps, I wear my best smile,
Trading troubles for humor, it's all just worthwhile.
So let's paint our tales with a wink and a jest,
In this playful exchange, come join me—a fest!

Negotiating with Tomorrow

Rang up tomorrow with coins from today,
Bartered for giggles in a whimsical way.
Chased shadows of worries, made offers to fate,
Exchanging the mundane for dance and a plate.

The clock ticked a bargain I couldn't ignore,
Each tick was a price drop, a mystery galore.
I tossed in my troubles, they kicked back a tune,
Underneath stars, while we haggled till noon.

Wheeling and dealing with smiles by my side,
Tomorrow was brightly adorned, full of pride.
Each plan was a joke with a punchline so keen,
I traded my doubts for some silly routine.

So here's to the joys that we captured this hour,
Together we'll flourish, let's barter our power.
For every tomorrow that's clad in pure glee,
Let's celebrate deals that keep setting us free!

Features and Flaws

In this store, you'll find some gems,
Shiny trinkets, strange little hems.
With features bold and flaws quite stark,
Even laughter leaves a mark.

A bargain hunter's crazy chase,
With socks that dance and spoons that race.
Buy one thought, get two for free,
Losing sense seems to be the key.

The items here are quite absurd,
Like clockwork birds without a word.
A philosophy that's half a laugh,
You'll find deep truths within the gaff.

So come on down, and take a peek,
At wisdom's humor, so unique.
They'll say you paid, but really, no,
For what's a cost when smiles can flow?

Mispriced Moments

Moments stacked like chips in stores,
Price tags marked, but who keeps scores?
You'll find a smile now marked down low,
And laughter's worth, we do not know.

A fleeting glance, a wink, a cheer,
All mispriced, but still so dear.
Like vintage jokes in thrifted shelves,
Where memories play, but not ourselves.

Oh, the deals on good old times,
Discounts on those silly rhymes.
A chuckle may cost very little,
Yet brings a joy that's far from brittle.

So grab a moment, take it home,
Make it yours, let out a groan!
For mispriced moments come and go,
But the fun you keep, it tends to glow.

The Essence of Return

Return your frowns, or trade regrets,
For joyful tears and silly bets.
We have a section on heartfelt glee,
And nonsense sold at half a fee.

This counter's stacked with second chances,
Where laughter blooms and silliness dances.
Exchanges made with hefty smiles,
Wisdom packed in pun-filled piles.

Find your essence among the racks,
Of quirky thoughts and laughter's tracks.
Refunds of joy are on the way,
Just sign the form, and choose your play.

So step right up and grab a giggle,
Unpacking truth that makes you wiggle.
For the essence here is crystal clear,
A testament to folly and cheer.

Scrapbook of Choices

In this scrapbook of wild delight,
Choose a memory, hold on tight.
Each page a twist, a turn of fate,
With laughter penned, it's never late.

Options blink like neon lights,
Reflections of our curious nights.
Decisions scribbled, some crossed out,
Yet every choice brings joy, no doubt.

Confetti dreams and wild ambitions,
Scattered thoughts in bright renditions.
Flip the pages, see what's near,
A quirky landscape of fun and cheer.

So take your pick, there's no wrong turn,
In life's grand book, there's much to learn.
With each good choice, we laugh and play,
In this scrapbook of choices, come what may.

Slashing Expectations

Grab a bargain on your dreams,
Cut the price, slash the seams!
Wishes wrapped in gift-wrapped fluff,
But hey, they're both short and tough.

Thoughts on sale, just take a look,
One-liners in every nook.
Buy one laugh, get two more free,
Returns accepted, just let me be!

Perks of living on discount shelf,
Who needs wisdom? Just ask yourself!
Pick some regrets—half off, today!
Join the club; we laugh and play.

Come, one, come all, to this great fair,
Where meaning's cheap, but we all care!
Grab your pen, write your rules,
In this bazaar, we're all just fools!

The Inventory of Experience

Check the aisles for outdated thrills,
Take home wisdom, void of frills!
A pet rock here, a mantra there,
Wrap it up, who'd even care?

Second-hand struggles in every pack,
Lessons learned, no need to hack.
Bargain bins piled high with schemes,
Trade your nightmares for sunny dreams.

Dusty novels filled with tales,
Whisk you away on whimsy sails.
Life's a mix of old and new,
For a nickel, you'll find your view.

Find delight in discount days,
Collective laughter pays in rays!
So here's to odds and ends galore,
In this shop, we all explore!

Potential in the Outlets

Voltage high in this strange bazaar,
Power surges, see how far!
Tap into dreams on a budget mode,
Just don't trip on the overload.

Bright ideas with sticky tags,
Grab 'em quick, before they lag!
Outlets buzzing with hopes for sale,
In this current, we'll never fail.

Flashy discounts on where to go,
Can't believe the deals on flow!
Future's waiting with open arms,
Plug in now for all the charms.

So bring your wits, a laugh or two,
We're all just trying to break through.
Recharge your heart, no need to pout,
In this market, we'll scream and shout!

Old Books, New Insights

Dusty tomes on a clearance rack,
Wisdom whispers—'don't look back!'
Pages turning, stories unfold,
What's the price? Just the bold!

Quirky quotes, half-written scripts,
Breaks from life's relentless grips.
Trade stale thoughts for novel plans,
In this library, one understands.

Forgotten tales, half-spilled tea,
Lessons waiting—oh, what a spree!
Purchase smiles; they're on a roll,
Collect some joy to fill your soul.

So roam these aisles with silly glee,
In the margins, find your spree!
For in each book—a laugh or two,
Nice and cheap, just like a clue!

Emptied Vaults, Full Hearts

In a store filled with laughter, I trod,
Old dreams on sale, how odd!
A price tag hung on my silly grin,
I tossed my worries in a bin.

Bargains found in moments we share,
Who knew joy could come with a flair?
A clearance aisle for dreams set free,
In this shop, it's all about glee.

With pennies spent on hopes we weave,
The work of whims is hard to believe.
A cart full of giggles and silly starts,
Who knew we'd fill our emptied hearts?

Counting smiles like coins, I roam,
In this market of joy, I find my home.
Bartering with joy, it feels so right,
In this funny world, let's dance tonight!

The Economy of Existence

A sign at the door says 'Buy One, Get Two',
Existence is fishy, who knew?
Prices fall on laughs, it's hard to see,
What's for sale in the depths of me?

Quick sales on wisdom, a clearance spree,
For a nickel of joy, would you barter with me?
Buy happiness, trade sarcasm, only a dime,
In this bazaar, we all seek the prime.

Life's used like gum beneath our shoe,
But chew it sweet, that's what we do.
Mark it down for a deal so grand,
Existence is cheap, come grab my hand!

Haggling over tears with a grin so wide,
Let's trade yesterday for today's joyride.
In this marketplace, everything's fair,
Laughter, my currency, just take your share!

Markdown Moments

Markdowns on joy, I check the tags,
Discounted hopes, no time for gags.
Half off the worries, buy now, don't wait,
It's a limited offer, why hesitate?

With every giggle, the prices drop,
Silly thoughts in a delightful shop.
I fill my cart with dreams on sale,
In this funny world, we cannot fail.

A price cut on care, take heart today,
Smiles on clearance, come out and play!
Moments for pennies that brighten the gloom,
In the aisles of laughter, joy is in bloom.

So gather your coins, let's make a deal,
Chasing the moments that make us feel.
In this market of laughs, grab what you see,
At a markdown of fun, come dance with me!

Experience for Sale: Take It or Leave It

Step right up to the wacky show,
Experiences in jars, just so you know.
A whiff of laughter, a taste of cheer,
Take it or leave it, the choice is clear!

A sprinkle of chaos, a dash of play,
You'll never find deals like these today.
Moments in bubbles, pinches of fate,
What's in your cart? Can't be too late!

Hours of joy for just a few ticks,
Exchange your troubles, the ultimate fix.
A giggle a day keeps the blues away,
Fill up your bag; who cares what they say?

So grab your pals, it's time to explore,
With silly experiences, who could want more?
Take life as it comes, with all of its quirks,
For laughs are the treasure, the best of the perks!

The Tangible Escapade of Living

Grab a ticket, it's a show,
A juggling act, just so you know.
We offer laughs, a tickle or two,
For a modest price, just for you.

Clowns in suits, they sell you doubts,
With every giggle, your worry shouts.
Hurry up, don't miss this chance,
To dance with chaos, in a silly trance.

Life's a fair at bargain rates,
Discounted woes, we tempt the fates.
Grab your cart, let's hit the booth,
For humorous twists, and twisted truth!

So come on down, partake the jest,
In this economy, we laugh the best.
The ticket's cheap, the fun is free,
Why not dawdle in absurdity?

Scraps of Meaning in the Margin.

Found a note in a dusty drawer,
'Happiness is just a penny store.'
So I pocketed it without a fuss,
Now I'm chasing giggles on the bus.

Coffee spills on my deep, profound,
Can't find wisdom on this merry-go-round.
Irony's rich, life's cheap thrill,
Yet it's the silly that gives a chill.

Cataloged dreams in a tattered book,
Endearing thoughts, if you just look.
Life's a puzzle with missing pieces,
Yet laughter, it surely never ceases.

So let's collect these scraps of glee,
For the wacky and wild are my cup of tea.
Dust off the nonsense, let's have a laugh,
In this margin of chaos, we'll find our path.

Bargain Bin Reflections

I rummaged through the thrift store shelves,
For wisdom lost, or thoughts of elves.
Found a mirror with a crooked smile,
Reflected hopes, though off by a mile.

A price tag on the joy we seek,
Half-off riddles for the meek.
The world is cluttered with bizarre finds,
Chasing meaning with whimsical minds.

Frayed edges, a tale that's half-told,
Sold as wisdom, but feels so bold.
Grab your shopping cart, take a ride,
Through aisles of laughter, let dreams collide.

So, if you seek true reason bare,
Check the bin, there's fortune to share.
The laughs may sell at cutdown rates,
But joy resides in the strangest crates.

Discounted Dreams.

Marked down hopes, they're on aisle three,
With a clearance sign so bright and free.
A sprinkle of chaos, a dash of charm,
Get your quirky dreams without the qualm.

Throw in some giggles, they're just next door,
Clumsy attempts to settle the score.
Overlooked visions, half-hearted schemes,
Who knew humor came in discounted dreams?

Toss the junk, take home the jest,
For laughter's the answer we love best.
In this marketplace of whims and schemes,
Find your treasure among the beams.

So let's trade our thoughts for a whiff of fun,
Under the sun, when the day is done.
These discounted dreams are meant to sell,
With laughter waiting, all is swell!

The Unmarked Cost of Joy

In a thrift shop of dreams, I roam,
Searching for giggles, but find a comb.
With smiles on clearance and laughter on hold,
There's a price tag on joy, but the ink's gone cold.

I barter with chuckles, swap frowns for cheer,
A coupon for happiness, it has disappeared.
At the checkout of silly, I can't find my change,
Did the price go up? Or is it just strange?

The cash register jingles, but what does it say?
Is joy on sale, or just lost in the fray?
I'll trade you my worries, they're dusty and old,
For a sparkle of laughter, some fun to behold.

With a wink and a grin, I'll take all I can,
Trading nonsense for gigs with a whimsical plan.
For a penny for giggles, I'll gladly pay twice,
In this market of mirth, where we barter for spice.

Expired Wisdom at Rock Bottom

At the bottom of wisdom, I found a few jars,
Full of old quotes and some faded old scars.
Buying regrets at a price that seems steep,
But I'll empty my pockets for laughter so cheap.

Here's a lesson in folly, ten cents for a laugh,
A bargain with hindsight, on life's crazy path.
The wisdom is stale, like bread past its date,
But it's wrapped in a smile, so I'll call it fate.

I sift through these trinkets, mismanaged ideas,
Like mismatched socks and some outdated cheers.
I'll take this old nonsense, and one quirky thought,
For a song in the night that I can't help but trot.

At the end of the aisle, there's joy on the shelf,
With a label that says, "It's good for yourself!"
I'll buy these strange lessons, mix laughter with pain,
At the back of this store, there's sunshine in rain.

Dollar Store Destiny

In the aisle of cheap dreams, I find my way,
With my cart of wishes, both silly and play.
There's purpose in packets, each one just a dime,
But the value I'm searching for isn't worth a rhyme.

I gather up hopes in a plastic bag,
Mixed with snippets of joy that some others may snag.
A destiny shrunk to fit on a shelf,
But the price of a chuckle is worth more than wealth.

With fortunes on clearance, I've loaded my cart,
Trading moments for memories, a most fun-filled art.
The signs say "one size fits," which we know isn't true,
Yet I buy up the laughter—oh, what can I do?

The checkout line holds all my treasures so small,
In this dollar store world that can tangle us all.
With each quirky find, my spirit takes flight,
For when joy costs so little, it surely feels right.

The Last Chance Emporium

In an emporium bright with misfits galore,
I wander through aisles where the oddest things score.
With treasures marked down, and sales that entice,
I'll barter my troubles for a dab of good spice.

A sign says, "Last Chance" in glittering gold,
But the bargains I'm seeking are never quite sold.
With quirks that are quirky and whirligigs, too,
I'll buy a new laugh for a laugh that's not new.

They offer wise wisdom wrapped up as a joke,
With a side of confusion and nonsense to stoke.
I'll fill up my basket with giggles and glee,
For in this last chance place, I'm as happy as can be.

So come one, come all, to the wacky bazaar,
Where puns hang in shadows and gags shine like stars.
With a wink to the world as I stroll through the door,
I'll take home the laughter—who could ask for more?

Second-Hand Verities

Worn-out truths on display,
Dusty shelves, come what may.
Ponder carefully, take a look,
They might just be in your book.

Caution: may contain some flaws,
Buyer beware, check the claws.
Living wisdom, slightly used,
A bargain sale, you'll be amused.

Faded promises, one size fits all,
Try them on, you might just fall.
No need for rush, enjoy the show,
Life's little secrets, one big 'whoa!'

Charming quirks and purple prose,
Things you'll love and some you'll loathe.
Take a chance, don't hesitate,
Your second-hand fate awaits the gate.

Repurposed Reflections

Mirrors cracked with tales untold,
Glimpse your past, it's somewhat bold.
Recrafted joys in thrift store lights,
Chasing laughs on dizzy nights.

Memories squeezed in jars so tight,
Whipped cream dreams in morning light.
Buy a giggle, sell a sigh,
Rewind time, give it a try.

Old ideas stitched into new seams,
Once we danced, now we just dream.
Fish for wisdom, toss a lure,
In this market, rest assured.

Wrap your thoughts like fragile glass,
Tread gently, let the laughter pass.
Life's a circus, tickets half-price,
Step right up—oh, how nice!

Rusty Mementos for Sale

Old can openers, rusty and brown,
With a story of ups and downs.
Buy a memory, lose a tear,
Cheap nostalgia, loud and clear.

Worn-out shoes with miles to share,
Sole sisters, hang a prayer.
Whispers echo in every crease,
Step into comfort, feel the peace.

Faded postcards from times long past,
Cherished laughter that's built to last.
Vintage thoughts with a price tag,
Sometimes truth can make you wag.

Peruse the shelves, oh, what a find!
The past is yours, intertwined.
Just don't try to fix what's bent,
Rusty treasures are heaven-sent.

Dream States on Layaway

In a shop of wishful sleeps,
Tick the boxes, count the leaps.
Layaway dreams, all pre-owned,
In used tomorrows, hope is honed.

Bargain basement, lullabies,
Pick a nightmare, wear it wise.
Dancing with shadows through the night,
Maybe then, you'll see the light.

Whimsical thoughts, half-priced delight,
On discount racks, wrong becomes right.
How much fun can you possibly lend?
Just enough for a quirky blend.

Unlock the charm of sleep's embrace,
Aged dreams waiting in this space.
Checkout line of silly thoughts,
On layaway, we find our spots.

Flea Market Philosophies

Gather 'round, folks, come take a peek,
Buy wisdom cheap, with a side of critique.
Philosophy's here, on sale today,
No receipts given, in a quirky way.

Bargains in thought, just a dollar a dream,
Existential musings, or so it may seem.
Pick a plush thought, no need for a fight,
Every item comes with a laugh and a bite.

Trinkets of wisdom, piled high on the racks,
Pondering infinity while buying some snacks.
Life's quirky truths, offered with a grin,
In this marketplace, where do we begin?

Haggling over what makes us whole,
Wrapped in bargains, they're all on a roll.
Come find your purpose, it's deeply absurd,
Just don't ask for clarity, the price is unheard.

The Price of Existence

Welcome, dear shoppers, to the sale of your days,
Discounted emotions in curious displays.
What's the cost of a smile? Just two cents, my friend,
If you buy in bulk, the joys never end.

Buy one meaning, get two joys for free,
Life's just a shop where we barter and plea.
A slice of purpose, don't break the bank,
Just sign where it says, and you'll get a prank.

Check the aisles for your dreams on a shelf,
Grab an illusion, it's better than self.
Pick up a giggle and a frown for a dime,
Tell me what you need; we even have rhyme!

Existence is funny, come take it in stride,
Load up your cart, there's room for your pride.
But beware of regrets, they may cost you a pound,
Bargain or trade; it's a whimsical round.

Half-Off Heartstrings

Fifty percent off, all feelings on sale,
Grab a tender moment; don't let it go stale.
A half-baked romance, now just a sweet deal,
Try a heart built of laughter; it's truly ideal.

Swap hugs for handshakes; it's hip and it's cool,
Emotions on clearance, it's one wacky school.
With a smile for a quarter, it's hard to resist,
Yet tangled connections—oh wait, what's that twist?

A bargain for nostalgia is waiting in line,
But yesterday's heartstrings don't work out just fine.
Take a chance on the laughter, skip sorrow's long queue,
In this shop of emotions, there's plenty to do.

So cartwheel through aisles of affection and cheer,
With a discount on joy, who can shed a tear?
For happiness scattered, like leaves in the wind,
Grab life's funny moments, where wisdom may bend.

Auctioning the Soul

Step right up, folks, it's the ultimate show,
Bid on a soul, let your wild spirit flow.
Starting at one, can I get two for laughs?
The auction of dreams, where everyone quaffs.

Look at the sparkle, behold the delight,
A glimmer of hope in the soft, moonlit night.
Raise your paddles for purpose, don't miss this chance,
In a room full of whimsy, let's all do a dance.

The starting price drops for a tale full of fun,
Two bucks for a giggle, when all's said and done.
Place your bets wisely, on who can be bold,
In this quaint little market, our stories unfold.

When the gavel comes down, what will you have bought?
A piece of the universe, or just one silly thought?
In the auction of essence, don't let laughter fade,
Join in on the fun; with our dreams, be unmade.

Unraveled Threads of Significance

In the bargain bin of the mind,
Ideas jumbled, hard to find.
Discount dreams on every shelf,
Grab a thought, but keep yourself.

Wisdom packed in cardboard boxes,
Tangled truths wear fuzzy socks.
Happiness? Oh, it's half-price,
Just add a dash of silly spice.

Glimmers of joy peek from the rack,
Is it a gift, or a gimmick pack?
Philosophies at clearance rates,
Shop for smiles, avoid debates!

So fill your cart with whims and quirks,
In this store of zany works.
Who needs depth when fun's on sale?
Join the chaos, set your sail!

Traded Influences

Barter thoughts with quirky glee,
Trading smiles, we all agree.
Pass the nonsense, hold the weight,
Swap your doubts for something great.

On the corner, wisdom's street,
Silly slogans, catchy beat.
Exchanging musings like a game,
Who knew truths could be so tame?

Plato's thoughts for bubble gum,
Riding highs and feeling dumb.
With each trade, a laugh or two,
Sell absurdity, buy some hue!

Hold that color, bright and clear,
In this market, shed your fear.
Why be serious, let's be bold,
A barter's worth is made of gold!

The Auction of Aspirations

Step right up, the gavel's raised,
Bids for dreams, the crowd's amazed.
A vision here, a hope or two,
But watch your wallet, watch your view!

"Who'll give a dollar for a wish?"
Laughter echoes, dreams we dish.
Fate's on sale, what a steal,
Make a wager, spin the wheel!

Got a prayer, throw it in,
Maybe luck is due to win.
With every shout, the price goes up,
Raise your hand, don't spill your cup!

The auctioneer keeps the show anew,
Selling futures, both old and few.
But when the dust begins to clear,
You'll find a giggle holds the prize here!

Cheapened Epiphanies

Oh, the moments that we chase,
Cheapened truths all over the place.
Here's a nugget, only a dime,
Laugh it off, it feels like rhyme.

A "eureka" bought with coupons bright,
While wisdom dances out of sight.
Slap a sticker on your thought,
Sale on insight, take a shot!

Discount answers on the rack,
Philosophy in a paper sack.
Grab a lesson, real or fake,
In this market, what's at stake?

So let's embrace these coined confusions,
Find laughter in strange conclusions.
Who needs depth when it's all for fun?
In this bazaar, we've all just won!

Value Tags on Existence

In the clearance section where hopes reside,
You'll find a price tag, a quirky guide.
"One joy, two tears — a steal at this rate!"
Come shop for your dreams, won't you, mate?

A coupon for laughter, a markdown for pain,
Discounted regret, oh what a gain!
Here's a basket of wishes, all colors and sizes,
Grab one for yourself, no need for surprises!

The checkout clerk smiles, 'What's your choice today?"
Do you want happiness or just the display?
With a wink and a nod, you empty your soul,
For a quarter of fun, you can feel really whole!

So browse through the aisles, take your time, dear friend,
In this wacky bazaar, the deals never end.
For a penny of laughter, you might find it clear,
That value in chaos is the best souvenir!

The Discounted Purpose

Peering at prices on purpose to find,
A sale on intentions, oh what a kind!
"Half off your goals, just add some flair!"
Who's to say living's beyond repair?

An expiring batch of hopes weekly reduced,
Grab your own slice, don't let it go unused!
A lightning deal on dreams, but be wary my friend,
For some must be sealed, and no refunds to send!

Sample a vision, just a bite to taste,
An all-you-can-eat of whimsy and haste.
The cashier laughs softly, "It's all on display,
Find what you fancy, don't throw it away!"

So roll up your sleeves and dig through the racks,
There's purpose in clumsiness, no need to relax.
The joys that you stumble upon may surprise,
Like socks with blue stripes await your own eyes!

Bargain Bin of Dreams

Dive in the bin, where ambitions lie low,
A treasure trove hidden, come see what will show!
"Faded potential? Just a dollar a piece!"
The label says, "Act fast, dreams do not cease!"

A twisted ambition, a whimsical chart,
All stitched together, yet torn at the heart.
Bring cash for the laughter, a wallet for fun,
Who knew that existence is just a good pun?

Unruly ambitions, like socks without mates,
A handful of wishes amidst some debates.
Leave your worries behind, come take a good peek,
In this bizarre realm, laughter finds you unique!

Bargain bins sparkle, like stars in the night,
A haven for dreamers, each one shines bright.
So find your best deal on a laugh that will bubble,
In the sea of absurdity, there's no time for trouble!

Flea Market Philosophy

Wandering through stalls of thought and of cheer,
Funny how wisdom is stacked up right here.
"Ten bucks for a thought that's seen better days!"
Yet people all gather, in curious ways.

Wrapped in odd packages, truths you can find,
A jigsaw of nonsense, so perfectly aligned.
"Take two for the price of your sanity lost!"
Who knew that reflection could come at such cost?

On dusty old tables, ideas may clash,
Echoes of laughter with each crazy dash.
So barter your burdens; it's all in your head,
In this circus of living, all rules have been shed!

Flea market philosophers, wearing bright hats,
Trade quips for good vibes, and converse with the cats.
A platform for joy, a stage for delight,
For finding the funny, you don't need a light!

What Dreams May Cost

I sold my dreams for just a dime,
They promised gold but lacked the shine.
A wish on sale, all wrapped in twine,
I haggled hard, oh what a crime!

The vendor grinned, a sly old fox,
With laughter loud and mismatched socks.
"Just take a leap, but mind the rocks!"
And off I skipped, a paradox.

A fortune found in cotton candy,
With sprinkles bright, but far too dandy.
I thought I'd find my dreams quite handy,
But all I got was something randy!

So here I stand, a bargain bin,
With dreams for sale, where to begin?
A coffee mug that claims to win,
But all it brewed was silly grin!

The Art of Letting Go

I tried to hold on to my last piece of cake,
But it vanished quick, oh what a mistake!
I learned to let go, for goodness' sake,
As crumbs danced 'round like a wild mountain quake.

My worries piled like laundry unclean,
I tossed 'em out, oh what a scene!
They flew like kites, bright and keen,
And left me feeling rather serene.

The old regrets? A yard sale feast,
With laughter they went, to say the least.
Turned baggage to treasure, now I'm released,
To find new joys, like a happy beast!

So here's my mantra: let it all flow,
With every giggle, let's put on a show.
For life's too short to don a heavy toe,
We'll spin and twirl, and let the fun grow!

Soulmates for Sale

Two hearts on discount, don't take it too grim,
With chocolate eyes and a penchant for whim.
Bought at a price that seemed ever so slim,
We bicker and laugh, and dance on a whim.

A soulmate's listed, but what's in the box?
With coupon clippings, and mismatched socks.
"A deal of a lifetime!" the ad really rocks,
But all I got was a parrot that mocks!

So here we are, a quirky pair,
With love sold cheap, but we make a fair share.
Sharing our dreams in an old armchair,
With laughter and joy, we're quite the rare fare.

So if you're looking for hearts to embrace,
Come peruse our selection, it's a wild chase!
With giggles and goof-ups, oh what a space,
A soulmate for sale, come join the race!

Finding Gold in the Gutter

I stumbled upon a shiny old ring,
In a puddle where raindrops dance and sing.
I cleaned it off, but to my chagrin,
It was a toy, not the treasure I bring.

Yet in the mud, I saw sparkles bright,
A piece of gum gave me quite a fright.
A dollar bill ran off in the night,
Chasing my laughter, oh what a sight!

I scrunched up my nose, but I couldn't stay mad,
For each little find just made me feel glad.
In gutters of life, where dreams seem so bad,
I learned that the silly can never be sad!

So when you wander, take a good look,
For treasures await like a favorite book.
In dirt and in muck, don't let your heart cook,
You'll find gold in laughter, just take a second nook!

www.ingramcontent.com/pod-product-compliance
Lightning Source LLC
Chambersburg PA
CBHW051656160426
43209CB00004B/915